Analytical Thinking: Reproducible Exercises

Dr. Marlene Caroselli

HRD Press, Inc. • Amherst • Massachusetts

Published by: HRD Press, Inc.
22 Amherst Road
Amherst, MA 01002
1-800-822-2801 (U.S. and Canada)
413-253-3488
413-253-3490 (fax)
www.hrdpress.com

ISBN 978-1-61014-358-5

Production services by Jean S. Miller
Cover design by Eileen Klockars
Editorial services by Sally Farnham

Analytical Thinking

Overview: Participants will work in small groups on a number of problems that call for careful analysis. Each group will then create a checklist of steps to be taken when corporate crises occur.

Objective:
- To provide practice with problems requiring critical thinking.
- To ascertain the steps involved in the "damage-control" process.

Supplies:
- Copies of Worksheet 1-1, one per participant
- Overhead projector
- Five or six blank transparencies
- Pens for writing on transparencies

Time: 35–45 minutes

Advance Preparation: Make copies of Worksheet 1-1. Put tables and chairs into formations that allow four or five participants to work together.

Participants/ Application: This exercise, which works with any number of participants, can be employed at any time during the instructional day. As an opener, it stimulates collaboration among participants and underscores the need for participants to use critical thinking throughout the training session (no matter the topic). As an energizer, it is a good change-of-pace activity, bound to re-awaken interest because of its real-world familiarity. As a session-closer, it reinforces the need for participants to think analytically when they return to the workplace, where crises invariably occur.

Introduction to Concept:

The unofficial "Wizard of Spin" is Michael Sitrick, who is best known for his crisis management resolutions. If ever a situation requires critical thinking, it is when a crisis has erupted and needs to be contained. Companies that take action without analysis can put their very existence into jeopardy. Sitrick cites the case of the executive who denied a reporter's implication that the company was having trouble paying its vendors. His denial was based on truth—the company was *not* having cash flow problems. Vendors were receiving monies that were due them. However, when the story broke, the denial caused vendors to wonder if perhaps they were about to start receiving late payments. The company wound up bankrupt.

The spin doctor would have advised the executive to ask the reporter which vendors were making this claim. The executive could have then uncovered the actual problem and could have reported that to the journalist—probably the same day. In the interim, he could have given the journalist the names of dozens of other vendors who were satisfied with payment schedules.

There are many ways to report truth. But for a cynical public, the most believable truths are usually not those that claim un-truths are untrue. Today, you and your teammates will have an opportunity to play CEO-for-a-day. After specifying how you would react to each of these real-world scenarios, you will formulate a plan of action for crisis situations in general.

Procedure:

1. Distribute Worksheet 1-1. Allow 15 to 20 minutes for small groups to complete the assignment.

2. Have each small group join another small group to exchange action plans and then to prepare a composite action plan, synthesizing the best of each original. The synthesized plans will be printed on a blank transparency.

3. Have a spokesperson from each group of 8–10 present their action plans to the group at large.

4. Share with the class the fact that all of the case studies actually happened to Procter and Gamble, Chesterfield, and General Foods, and were handled with varying degree of "critical" success.

Extending the Activity:

1. Interview the CEO of the organization sponsoring the training you are presenting. Learn about crises that have arisen in the organization's history. Use these as the basis for a comparable worksheet.

2. Invite the head of a public relations firm to the class to critique the action plans the teams have created.

Workplace Connections:

1. Ask each participant, upon his or her return to work, to fashion a response to this question: "What is the worst thing that could happen here?" Next, he or she should describe the steps that would prevent the crisis or, if it is unavoidable, to outline the steps that would reduce the severity of the consequences. These plans should then be shared with upper management if comparable plans do not already exist.

2. Encourage post-class benchmarking to learn what plans other organizations have in place.

Questions for Further Consideration:

1. If the head of your organization were to do your job for just one day, what would he or she learn? What would most surprise the person?

2. How prepared do you feel your organization is for crises in the workplace?

A. Assume you are the head of a successful company that produces household products. Suddenly, you find the entire country talking about your logo, a moon with starts clustered around it. The talk has an ugly tone—people are saying the symbol represents Satan. You fear the public will lose faith in your product. On the other hand, you have worked hard to achieve that well-recognized corporate identity. What specific steps would you take to battle the rumors?

1) _____
2) _____
3) _____
4) _____
5) _____

B. It is 1934. You are CEO of a cigarette company. While you know that heavy cigarette smoking produces a bad cough in some smokers, you are certain smoking does not produce leprosy. Nonetheless, a rumor is rapidly spreading that your company in Richmond, Virginia has employed a leper and that people who smoke the cigarettes he has touched are getting leprosy. What, specifically, would you do to counter these untruths?

1) _____
2) _____
3) _____
4) _____
5) _____

C. The new product, a carbonated candy, looked like a dream come true. Soon after its introduction, however, stories began to travel across the country that the candy exploded in the digestive system. What would you do to counter the false claims of sickness and death?

1) _____
2) _____
3) _____
4) _____
5) _____

D. Having considered three specific scenarios, prepare an action plan detailing what steps should be followed, generally speaking, when crises occur at your company.

1) _____
2) _____
3) _____
4) _____
5) _____

Overview: This activity presents participants with a number of problems, the solution to which requires the ability to spot trends or patterns. Extending this kind of thinking, participants will be asked to consider emerging trends in the world of business.

Objective: To strengthen analytical skills.

Supplies:
- Slide 2-1
- Equipment for showing PowerPoint slides
- Flipchart
- Token prize (optional)

Time: About 25 minutes

Advance Preparation: Purchase a small prize if you have decided to use such. Make the transparency. Write the two examples from the Introduction on the flipchart but keep them covered until they are needed.

a)   1 10 3 9 5 8 7 9 6 ___ ___

b)   8 10 36 92 256 696 ___

Arrange seating, if the room permits, so table groups of four or five can work together.

Participants/ Application: The best times to use this exercise with groups are at the beginning of the training session and at the end. As a warm-up, it enables small groups of participants to start working as a team from the very start of the class. It also establishes the context within which they will be working: in a challenging environment that requires them to do more than just sit passively and absorb information. In such a context, participants are expected to think about what they are learning and to form their own frames of reference.

   As a concluding exercise, the problems posed and the discussion prompted by them work to encourage thought about the future. For the immediate future, you can ask how participants will apply the training. For the more distant future, you can ask participants to consider the megatrends that futurists claim are already beginning to emerge.

Introduction to Concept:

Futurists John Naisbitt and Patricia Aburdene encourage us to think about the information we receive on a daily basis and what it is really telling us. To learn what it is really telling us means we must spot and carefully analyze the trends that seem to be emerging. Critical thinking of this type requires time, comparison, and lots of questions. If we are unwilling to engage in such tought-provocative action, however, we may truly find ourselves shocked by the future.

Engaging in simple pursuits often allows us to establish the framework within which more complicated analysis can occur. Developing the ability to discern patterns sharpens the skills of analysis and can lead to valuable insights, such as identification of emerging trends. An example of a small-scale analysis task is this. [Show these examples, written on the flipchart, one at a time. Ask participants to guess what numbers come next in the series.

a) 1 10 3 9 5 8 7 7 9 6 ___ ___

b) 8 10 36 92 256 696 ___

Procedure:

1. After a few minutes, if participants still have not figured out the problems on the flipchart, share the answers. They are: a) **11** (because the odd numbers are increasing by 2 each time), and **5** (because the even number, 10, goes down by one each time) and b) **1904**, because two numbers are added together each time (8 + 10 = 18) and then multiplied by 2 to obtain the next number in the series (36). Next, 36 is added to 10, to obtain 46, which is then doubled to obtain 92, and so on.

2. Offer a token prize to the first participant who is able to repeat this sequence (or write it on the board) without referring to notes. [Allow enough time for at least one person to come to the front of the room to try writing the sequence from memory.]

105, 989, 184, 777, 063, 564, 942, 352, 821, 147

Most participants will set right to work attempting to memorize the numbers, when in fact there is a very powerful gimmick operating here: the numbers are organized in increments of seven. So all one really needs to do is remember where to end: at 105. Starting with 7 and adding seven each time will ultimately lead the token-prize winner to 105 (989, 184, 777, 063, 564, 942, 352, 821, 147).

Point out that data and information are not always organized so neatly for us, but when they are, we are able to recall the information quicker and more successfully.

3. Show Slide 2-1, noting that patterns are sometimes buried among numbers, sometimes among words, and sometimes by events themselves. Have groups of five or six participants work on the transparency problems, the answers to which are:

    1) The next letter is "N," continuing the spelling out of the numbers from 1 to 9.

    2) Share the answer: The numbers, if written as words, are alphabetically arranged. Then discuss the need to go beyond the obvious, to move outside the box as we problem-solve.

    3) Christmas, because there is no "l." [Noel]

    4) The same groups will then work to describe at least three trends they believe are emerging in their field, industry, world of business, or the economy itself. They should, whenever possible, back up their opinions with statistics.

    5) After 10 or 15 minutes, merge two groups and have them share the trends they have "spotted" with each other.

    6) Following this discussion, call on one spokesperson from each merged group to share the essence of their predictions.

7) Conclude the activity by encouraging participants to form their own frames of reference, based on carefully assimilated information and carefully constructed patterns. Acknowledge that these reference-points may have to be calibrated from time to time.

Extending the Activity:

1. Sometimes misunderstanding prevents us from solving problems. Here is one example:

   In a good-sized metropolis of 350,488 citizens, 7% of the people in the greater metropolitan area have unlisted phone numbers. One night, as you thumb through the phone book, you choose three pages at random (containing a total of 900 names). How many of those will have unlisted numbers?

   The answer, of course, is zero, because if they are not listed, they will not be in the phone book in the first place. Invite participants to share other examples of times when misunderstanding caused problems to be created or to remain unsolved.

2. Use the stratification device to discern what patterns may be emerging among workplace issues; have participants quickly list 20 to 30 problems or concerns that come to mind when they think about work. Then have them analyze the list to find patterns, trends, or clusters.

Workplace Connections:

1. Suggest that employees meet on a regular basis to make predictions for the next three, six, and twelve months about their workplace, technology, and general trends in their business world, after the course concludes. Then encourage them to meet on the anniversary dates three, six, and twelve months later to learn whose predictions had the greatest accuracy. That person, perhaps, can be awarded the money others have put into a "prediction" pot.

2. Recommend that participants continue developing their trend-spotting skills by reading *Megatrends 2000* or a similar future-oriented book. They should discuss the ideas presented and the ideas they come up with at least one other person in the workplace.

Questions for Further Consideration:

1. What trends do you feel are emerging in terms of medical advances?

2. What trends do you believe are emerging in terms of our lifestyles?

3. What trends do you see emerging as far as the makeup of the workforce is concerned?

4. What trends do you foresee occurring in terms of technology?

5. What preparations is your organization making to be ready for these changes?

What comes next?

1) O   T   T   F   F   S   S   E   _____

   What is the pattern in this arrangement?

2) 86   11   4   90   1   7   16   12   28   2   _____

   What is the holiday?

3) A   B   C   D   E   F   G   H   I   J   K   L   M
   N   O   P   Q   R   S   T   U   V   W   X   Y   Z

2-1

Overview: Participants will begin by studying the Triple-A Approach and then using it to formulate a persuasive proposal on a workplace issue. The presentation will be evaluated by other class members.

Objective: To familiarize participants with the Triple-A Approach to presenting information.

Supplies:
- Slide 3-1
- Equipment for showing PowerPoint slides
- Scraps of paper

Time: Approximately 30 minutes

Advance Preparation: Cut up scraps of paper, six or seven for each participant.

Participants/ Application: Arrange for table groups of five or six to work together. This exercise works well as a session-opener (to illustrate that in training-session teams or on workplace teams or simply in everyday encounters, persuasion skills are indeed valuable) or as a change-of-pace activity that asks participants to critique what was learned thus far and to persuade others to accept their opinions regarding which elements of the instructional content are likely to have most relevance in the workplace.

Introduction to Concept:

Author Ken Blanchard asserts that "the key to successful leadership today is influence, not authority." We influence others by our example, to be sure, but also by our words—whether those words are delivered by speaking, by writing, or by the electronic medium. Sometimes, when we observe others who always seem to get what they want, we are envious or puzzled by the apparent magic they exert over others. In truth, though, the persuaders we admire have finely tuned their communication skills.

One tool that will assist you in your effort to make a point and influence others to accept your viewpoint is the Triple-A Approach. It focuses on three factors. [Show Slide 3-1 now and briefly discuss the elements.]

Procedure:

1. Once participants have had a chance to review the transparency, divide the class into groups of five or six.

2. Assign each group one of the following topics to be developed using the Triple-A Approach. (You may choose other topics that may have special relevance for your participants. Or, if the activity is used as a concluding activity, the different groups will try to persuade others to adopt their point of view regarding which aspects of the training session were the most valuable.)

We should have a dress code at work.

Mondays and Fridays should be "dress-down days."

Secretaries should receive a percentage of their boss's annual bonus.

Employees should be able to evaluate their supervisors.

Employees should be allowed to use the Internet for personal business during slow periods.

3. Allow the teams about 20 minutes to write out their arguments and to select a spokesperson to deliver the written remarks.

4. Before or after the spokesperson attempts to persuade the other groups, distribute small sheets of paper. Upon the conclusion of each presentation, ask participants (other than members of the presenting group) to write one word on their papers: "Yes" (indicating the argument was persuasive) or "No" (indicating the argument did not influence their thinking).

5. Collect the scraps and pass them to the presenting group.

Extending the Activity:

1. Show a video of a well-known persuasive speech (such as the President's State of the Union address or a lawyer's closing argument) and analyze it as a group, using the factors in the Triple-A Approach as the criteria.

2. Invite the top salesperson from a local real estate firm to address the class on the reasons for his or her success in selling.

3. Ask small groups to create an acronym of their own for decision-making.

Workplace Connections:

1. Request that participants identify one individual in their workplace having the toughest decision of all to make. Then recommend that they meet with that person to learn more about the process of decision-making. Suggest that they make notes on the meeting, to be shared with the individual first and later with groups of employees.

2. Employees should reflect weekly on the percentage of time they spent at work absorbing knowledge, the percentage of time they spent developing new ideas, the percentage of time they spent implementing those ideas, and the percentage of time spent evaluating new ideas. A simple graphic will enable them to tell at a glance if they are maintaining a roughly equal division among the categories, such as this one:

% of time spent
absorbing knowledge

% of time spent
developing new ideas

% of time spent
evaluating ideas

% of time spent
implementing ideas

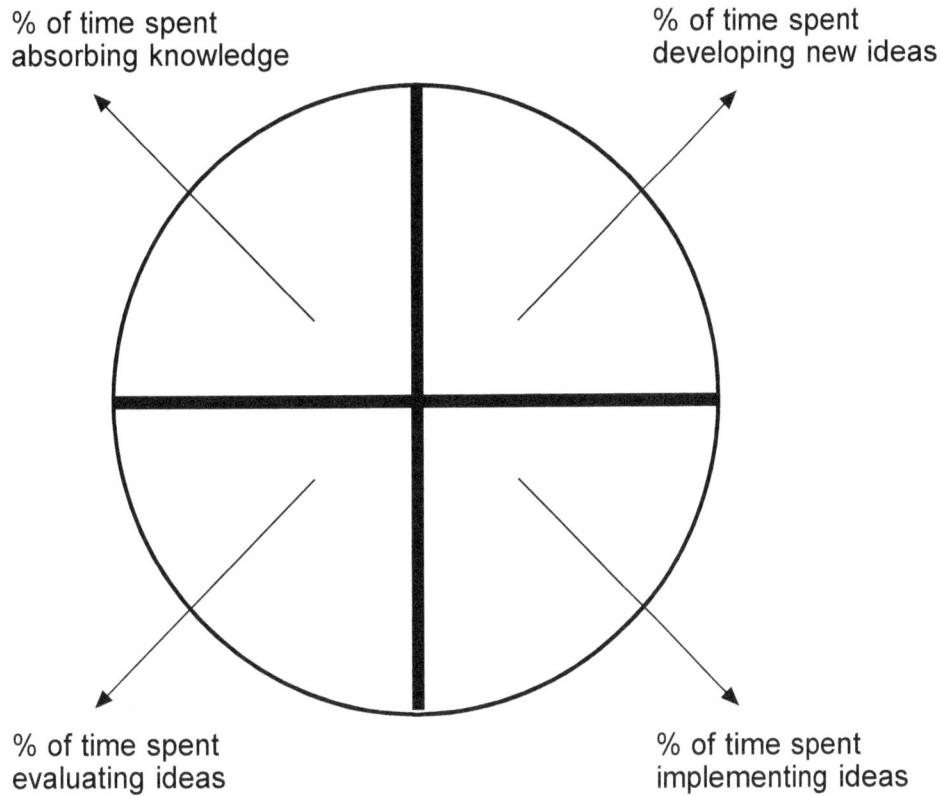

Questions for Further Consideration:

1. How much discussion is typically accorded decisions made in your workplace?

2. To what extent are employees invited to voice their opinions?

3. What factors do you take into account as you make decisions at work?

4. In terms of organizational or national history, what poor decisions can you recall prominent people having made? What elements went into the poor decision-making?

5. What works well in preventing "groupthink" from occurring?

Appeal	– to their emotions
	– to their WIFM need (What's in it for me?)
	– to their basic sense of decency/fairness
Anticipate	– their questions
	– their objections
	– their reactions
Ask	– for what you need
	– for commitment
	– for a chance to succeed

3-1

Overview:	After considering the definition and examples of metaphor, participants will create their own, based on common workplace concerns.
Objective:	To develop analytical thought by showing participants how to rephrase or convert a common problem to a metaphorical expression.
Supplies:	None required.
Time:	About 15 minutes
Advance Preparation:	Arrange seating to enable participants to work together in groups of four or five, if possible.
Participants/ Application:	Adaptable to any size group, this exercise fits into any part of the instructional day, as the issues participants will suggest will relate to whatever topic you are facilitating.

Introduction to Concept:

"To understand the metaphor," Aristotle wrote thousands of years ago, "is the beginning of genius." We find leaders in every field using metaphors to explain complex concepts in the simplest of ways. We also find ordinary people serving as metaphors. Rosa Parks, for example, has been referred to as a metaphor of societal changes occurring in the second half of the 20th century.

The world of international politics is rife with metaphorical allusions. Former Prime Minister Margaret Thatcher, for example, was often referred to as an "iron fist in a velvet glove." Winston Churchill, describing the power of Communism to separate the Eastern Bloc nations from the freedom Western Europe reveled in, called it the "Iron Curtain." Ronald Reagan, of course, shaped our thinking about Communism when he called it the "Evil Empire."

To depict the unspoken but very real prejudice women and minorities face, Anne Morrison coined the term "the glass ceiling." And Jesse Jackson, seeking to unify people of different races and different religions, invited them to join his "Rainbow Coalition." School children at Northside Elementary in Fairport, New York, projected their feelings about the coming school year in metaphoric terms:

- Middle school will be birth and funeral at the same time.
- Middle school is a jump from a waterfall—you might land in water, you might land on rocks.
- Middle school is a ride on the crest of a tsunami wave.
- Middle school is one key of a large keyboard.
- Middle school is a single step on life's staircase.

Procedure:

1. Define "metaphor" (a comparison between two things not usually compared) and explore the examples.

2. Divide the class into groups of four or five. Ask participants to list a fear or concern or problem facing them in particular or businesspeople in general. Compile on flipchart paper a list of all the issues.

3. Ask each group to select one issue from the posted list and describe it in metaphoric terms. State that groups will have 10 to 15 minutes to make the comparisons and to explain the rationale for them.

4. Have a spokesperson from each group read their metaphors aloud. Discuss with the class as a whole whether or not the presented example really is a metaphor.

5. Ask an outside judge to choose the metaphor he or she liked best and to tell the class why.

Extending the Activity:

1. Have participants discuss this metaphor from Peter Silas, CEO of Philips Petroleum: "We cannot afford to wait until the storm has passed. We must learn to work in the rain." Or this from management author/consultant Warren Bennis: "If I were to give off-the-cuff advice to anyone trying to institute change, I would ask, 'How clear is your metaphor?'"

2. Ask class members to find examples of metaphors in the newspaper.

3. Make copies of speeches delivered by famous people or organizational leaders and have participants find the metaphors in them.

Workplace Connections:

1. Recommend that participants collect business metaphors, such as this one by Peter Vaill, a professor at George Washington University: "Business life is permanent whitewater."

2. Encourage participants to develop their own metaphoric insights and use them as the occasions demand.

Questions for Further Consideration:

1. The story of "Alice in Wonderland" has been called a metaphor for business-as-we-know-it-today. How would you explain this comparison?

2. What metaphor would you use to describe your workplace?

Overview:	Participants will work with one or two others to figure out the answers to deceptively simple problems, designed to "fool" participants who do not analyze the questions carefully enough.
Objective:	To encourage participants to apply deliberate, critical thought to problem scenarios.
Supplies:	Copies of Worksheet 5-1 and 5-2, one per participant
Time:	About 20 minutes
Advance Preparation:	Prepare copies of the worksheets. Ideally, you can arrange seating so participants can work in pairs or triads.
Participants/ Application:	The questions on this worksheet activity are designed to fool the problem solver, in that the answers are not obvious but are definitely solvable. Any number of participants can work on this activity.

Introduction to Concept:

"There's this faculty in the human mind that hates any question that takes more than ten seconds to answer," author Norman Mailer once observed. We humans, especially we Americans, like to move. We like fast cars, time-saving machinery, and labor-saving devices. But when it comes to problems, we often move too fast, failing to give the situation the attention it deserves. Some problems, it is true, can be solved quickly. The majority, however, demand critical analysis rather than guesses. They ask problem-solvers to shift paradigms, to put assumptions aside, to deal in facts rather than conjecture.

The activity in which you will be engaged today has a number of problems for you. They are all solvable. However, they will take more than ten seconds to answer.

Procedure:

1. Distribute Worksheet 5-1 and allow about 10 minutes for completion.

2. Share the answers with participants:

   1) It may have been the apple, although there really is no evidence to suggest it was. The Bible simply refers to the fruit of "the tree of the knowledge of good and evil."

   2) Karloff played the monster created by Dr. Frankenstein.

   3) Leslie is Anthony's son.

4) The rearrangement of the matchsticks spells the word "nil," which, of course, means "nothing."

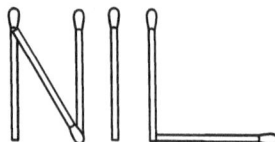

5) There were six managers representing four different professional organizations.

6) The answer is "G-I ants."

7) The answer is 28. (To help participants understand how the answer was arrived at, ask them to imagine the team members standing side by side. Team member A shakes hands with B, C, D, E, F, G, and H. That's a total of seven handshakes in the first round, because team member A is not shaking hands with himself. Then it is time for team member B. Remember, she has already shaken with A, so she shakes with C, D, E, F, G, and H, for a total of 6. Add the 7 and the 6 and you have 13 so far. Continue this way and you will get the final total of 28.)

8) Portland Trailblazers.

9) Skiing would be the penultimate experience. "Penultimate" means "next-to-the-last."

3. Distribute Worksheet 5-2 and allow a few minutes for participants to solve the mystery. (The reason Joe Saturday suspects Janice is that if Veronica had come home after Janice, Veronica's raincoat would have been on top, not Janice's.)

4. Wrap up the activity by leading a discussion regarding the kinds of things in the workday and workplace that are seen but overlooked and that could spell disaster if not attended to. Point out that Quality-meister Dr. Joseph Juran claims that American workers are so busy fighting fires that they no longer hear the alarm signals going off. Ask whether there are any alarm signals being set off in the workplace that we have been ignoring. Tie the question to events or people on the national scene who are sending out signals that we are ignoring.

Extending the Activity:

1. Have participants create a workplace mystery story of their own, in which an important clue is presented but not emphasized. The stories might center on a common problem a team is facing, for example, or a challenge with which a whole department is coping. They can exchange their stories and see how good the others were at analyzing the clues to solve the mystery.

2. Encourage a discussion of unexplained phenomena in the natural world often presented in television programs or videos ("Mysteries of the Seas," "Mysteries of the Universe," "Mysteries from the Animal Kingdom"), and puzzling events in the business world, as well. ("How does the European Commonwealth function as well as it does?")

Workplace Connections:

1. Recommend that a group of participants work as fund-raising volunteers to design a murder-mystery evening with employee-actors interacting with employee-guests.

2. Rent classic murder mystery movies, such as *Dial 'M' for Murder,* and show them over a several-day period at lunchtime. Ask for a volunteer to "moderate"—i.e., stopping the video at certain points to discuss the clues spotted up to that point.

Questions for Further Consideration:

1. What specific elements go into the creation of a good "whodunit"?

2. What mysteries have recently been solved in your workplace?

3. What mysteries still remain?

4. How can organizations tap into the pleasure employees find in reading a good mystery outside of work in order to generate excitement in solving a problem at work?

5. Is your own mystery-solving style a deductive or inductive one?

Directions: Working with one or two others, you will now have an opportunity to test your critical-thinking skills—especially your analytical skills—with these questions. Read them carefully, discuss them, and then write your answer in the blank space.

1. What fruit caused Adam and Eve to be banished from the Garden of Eden? _____

2. Boris Karloff is known around the world for his masterful portrayal of an abnormal character in the movies. What was the name of that character? _____

3. Assume that Leslie is a man. If Anthony's son is Leslie's father, what relationship is Leslie to Anthony? _____

4. How can you move only two matches so that you leave nothing in this existing row of six matches?

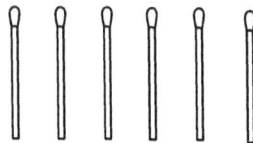

5. A group of managers, fully aware of the importance of networking, shared the following facts with each other:

    -   Each man belongs to exactly two professional organizations.
    -   Each organization is represented in the group by exactly three managers.
    -   Every possible pair of professional organizations has exactly one member of the group in common.

    How many managers are there in the group and how many different professional organizations are represented?

6. Combining a common verbal reference used to describe solders with a common bug, can you come up with the name of a National Football league team?

7. There are eight team members in a warehouse. Each shakes hands just once with each of the other members of the same team. What is the total number of handshakes?

8. Can you figure out which team in the National Basketball Association is represented by this sesquipedalian sequence: "Pathway pyromaniacs from a left-sided land?"

9. Joe has been daydreaming of ways to spend his upcoming vacation. Among his choices are scuba-diving, horseback riding, roller-skating along Muscle Beach, visiting relatives, attending a series of baseball games, skiing, and swimming in the Pacific. The choices are arranged in ascending order of preference. Knowing this, what would you say Joe regards as the penultimate experience?

Directions: Work with one or two others to solve the mystery presented here. All the clues you need are contained in the story.

Two newly hired customer service representatives have decided to room together. Things have been going well, both on the job and in their personal lives. But approximately two months after the two women moved in together, a tragedy occurred. Detective Joe Saturday was called to the scene in response to a 9-1-1 call at about six in the morning. Here's what happened when he got to the scene.

Janice Huerrerra, visibly shaken, let the detective in. Her roommate, Veronica Barclay, lay on the floor, a long-handled knife protruding from her chest. When the detective examined the body, he found that Veronica had been dead for several hours. He gave the apartment a cursory inspection, knowing the forensic technicians were on their way. He saw a knife missing from a rack of kitchen knives, bloody towels on the bathroom floor, and two raincoats on a chair. The top one had a .38 caliber gun sticking out of the pocket.

Before he could even ask about it, Janice admitted that the gun belonged to her but claimed she had a permit for it. Saturday then asked Janice about the events that led to her phone call to 9-1-1. She explained that she had been out on a date and returned about 10:30 p.m. She went right to bed after finding a note from her roommate saying she would not be in until 1:00 a.m. or 2:00 a.m.

The next thing she remembered was hearing Veronica come in, complaining about the rainstorms. She vaguely recalled hearing Veronica throw her raincoat on a chair and whisper to someone Janice assumed was her boyfriend. Then she heard Veronica in the bathroom. Just before she dozed off again, Janice heard Veronica's bedroom door close. She is certain, however, that she heard a man's laughter coming from Veronica's bedroom.

When Janice arose early the next morning, she found the body on the floor. In response to the detective's question, she assures him that she has not touched a thing, other than the phone to call 9-1-1.

The detective decides Janice is a suspect. On what basis? _____

_____

_____

Overview: Participants will be required to listen carefully so the correct information is received, and then to develop a strategy for solving a mystery.

Objective: To develop awareness of the importance of participation in collective problem-solving.

Supplies:
- Copies of Handout 6-1 (cut into strips)
- Flipchart

Time: 5–25 minutes

Advance Preparation: Write these words on the flipchart (but keep it covered until it is time for the exercise to begin):

- Who? [Ask, "Who was murdered?"]
- Weapon?
- Where?
- When? [Ask, "When did the victim die?"]
- Why?

Participants/ Application: **Note:** This exercise, although it can certainly stand alone, is an ideal follow-up to exercise #5, "A Foolery of Fun." Because of its interactive nature, however, it will be somewhat difficult for more than 25 and fewer than 10 participants to engage in it. It works best at the end of the training day because it offers the promise of an early dismissal to the teams that effectively employ analytical skills.

Introduction to Concept:

Problems are seldom solved in isolation in the workplace. With the vast majority of American firms using traditional, cross-functional and self-directed teams to continuously improve processes, the need for collective problem-solving assumes greater importance than ever before.

"Synergy" is the term that refers to the combined results of the "whole" team being greater than the sum of its individual parts. Without effective leadership, though, without a focus on the task, without positive interpersonal relationships, synergy may never be realized.

Procedure:

1. Start this activity 30 minutes before the normal ending time for the class. Explain that because participants have worked so hard to integrate concepts and assimilate new knowledge, you are going to reward them with a mystery story. They will be given all the clues they need to solve the mystery—which can actually be solved in five minutes. Warn them, however, that most teams take thirty minutes to solve the mystery. If they manage to complete it before the thirty minutes have elapsed, they are free to leave for the day.

2. Ask for two observers (more if it is a large class). Once the activity is underway, you can take the observers aside and ask them to note things like:

   1) Who assumed leadership? Was there evidence of conflict?

   2) How did the strategy for solving the mystery evolve?

   3) How well did participants listen to obtain the information they needed?

   4) What level of participation was evident among the members?

   5) Were they able to quickly overcome their confusion about the inequitable distribution of the clue strips?

   6) How well did they work as a team?

   Note: Because this activity produces a feverish pitch of excitement, it is anti-climactic to call the group together for the observer's debriefing immediately following their solving the mystery. Either begin the next day with the observer's report or—if the training session is a one-day program—use the observations for the benefit of the observers only.

3. Give these additional instructions:

   "If you are able to analyze the 'whisps' of information you are about to receive, you should be able to solve this crime within the next thirty minutes. You must figure out the answers to these questions."

   [Walk to the flipchart, point to each "W" word, and say it. For the first, however, be certain to say, *"Who was murdered?"* and not "Who was the murderer?" Be prepared to have someone insist later that you said, "Who was the murderer?"]

   "You cannot show the clues to one another. When you have your answers, write them on the flipchart. I will review them when you have all five. If they are all correct, you're outta here! If they are not all correct, I can only tell you how many are wrong—but not which ones."

   I cannot repeat these instructions, except to remind you that you will work together as a team and that you have all the information you need."

4. Distribute the clue strips, taking special care to give the six quietest members of the class the six clues written in capital letters—one each. (These are the most critical elements.) With the remaining strips, give some people none, some people just one, and others two.

5. If they have not solved the crime in 25 minutes, give them the answers.

Who?	Whisper
Weapon?	Marble statue of Erte figure
Where?	Whisper's apartment
When?	7:30 p.m.
Why?	She threatened to report Mayfield's hit-and-run accident to the police

Extending the Activity:

1. Invite a police detective to address the class regarding the use of analytical, deductive and inductive thinking in the solution of actual crimes.

2. Create reading comprehension exercises based on workplace documents. Select a paragraph. Ask participants to read it just once, and then to answer questions based on their understanding of what they have read.

Workplace Connections:

1. Encourage the post-class exploration of workplace mysteries by asking, "Why do so many managers forget to give recognition for good work?" "Why do so many employees feel supervisors are overpaid for what they do?" or "Why is 'communication' the number one problem in so many work sites?" Suggest that employees read current business books to find some of the answers.

2. Suggest that employees approach their supervisors about a weekly anonymous posting (to an actual bulletin board, an electronic one, or anonymously on 3" x 5" cards) with completions of this prompt: "It's a mystery to me why…." The supervisor will then take the responses and reply to them on a regular basis.

Questions for Further Consideration:

1. Discuss the importance of listening in an effective workplace.

2. What can happen to a group with two (or more) very strong leaders?

3. How important is teamwork to the outputs your work unit creates?

4. How effective is teamwork in your work unit?

5. What can a team leader do to encourage participation by all team members?

6. How frequently do you and your co-workers step back from your work and assess it to see if you are on the right track?

7. Can you think of situations in which hastiness prevailed over good sense in problem-solving?

8. Who is the best company problem-solver you know, and how did he or she get to be exemplary?

Clue Strips

SLY MAYFIELD STRUCK HIS LOVER REPEATEDLY WITH A MARBLE STATUETTE OF AN ERTE FIGURE.

SLY MAYFIELD PICKED UP THE STATUETTE AT 7:29 P.M.

SLY MAYFIELD PICKED WHISPER UP AT HER APARTMENT FOR A DINNER DATE.

WHISPER THREATENED TO REPORT MAYFIELD'S HIT-AND-RUN ACCIDENT TO THE POLICE.

WHISPER, A WORLD FAMOUS MODEL, WAS DEAD BY 7:30 P.M.

Unbeknownst to Mayfield, Whisper's brother died in a hit-and-run accident four years earlier.

Whisper was taking the fashion world by storm. Her jealous streak, though, was a problem.

Whisper's roommate was an airline stewardess named Gypsy.

Gypsy was having a secret affair with Sly Mayfield.

Gypsy left the apartment with her date, Tony Ackman, at 7:05 p.m.

Sly Mayfield arrived at the apartment at 7:10 p.m.

Whisper had learned from a former boyfriend, still in love with her, that Sly had been involved in a hit-and-run accident from which he had left the scene.

Sly Mayfield, still enraged, drove a knife through Whisper's heart at 7:35 p.m.

Neighbors heard screams and called the police, who arrived at 7:45 p.m.

The police dusted for fingerprints and forensic evidence until 8:30 p.m.

Tony Ackman, Wall Street financier, had met Whisper when she was shooting an ad on Wall Street.

Tony Ackman arrived at the apartment at 7:00 p.m.

Gypsy gave Tony Ackman a dry martini at 7:05 p.m.

Whisper had quarreled before with Sly about the hit-and-run accident.

Gypsy and Tony Ackman arrived at Le Bistro at 7:35 p.m.

Whisper suspected Gypsy was having an affair with Sly Mayfield.

Tony Ackman, slightly inebriated, quarreled with the maitre d' at the Bistro at 7:33 p.m.

Whisper's former boyfriend, Lieutenant Forrester of NYPD, was jealous of Sly Mayfield.

Overview: After a brief presentation of commonly used patterns, participants will work in pairs to prepare a written response to a given prompt, employing one organizational pattern.

Objective:
- To familiarize participants with the various organizational patterns that help in the assimilation and presentation of information.

- To give participants the opportunity to structure information around a specific pattern.

Supplies:
- Slide 7-1
- Equipment for showing PowerPoint slides

Time: About 20 minutes

Advance Preparation: If possible, arrange the seating so pairs can work together.

Participants/ Application: This exercise, which can be used with any size group, works well as an introductory or warm-up technique, affording participants the chance to learn about each other, each other's organizations, and the use of suitable patterns for presenting what they have learned. Ideally, the pairs will be composed of participants who do not know each other well, in which case they can discuss their respective departments or organizations, and then select one to write about. If they do know each other and/or if they are from the same organization, there will be more time spent on the writing than on the getting-to-know-you information.

Introduction to Concept:

How do we find the structure of framework that allows us to organize our thoughts in a meaningful way? The process of critically studying the materials to be presented leads us to the most suitable structure among many possible structures. There is seldom a singular "right" format for ordering our thoughts. Rather, the more familiar we are with the wide array of possibilities, the more likely we are to select the one that will work best given a number of circumstances (the background of the listening or reading audience; the desired length of the presentation or document; the purpose for which you are assembling information, etc.).

Let's say you have to write an article for a business journal or teach an in-house course on the topic of management. How would you organize the information you wanted to present? You could choose one of the following: [Show Slide 7-1 now.]

The Chronological Approach—This uses references to time. So, you might trace the evolution of various buzz-terms that characterized various management theories over the years, or you might discuss the historical events that came before what we are experiencing today.

The FDP (Famous Dead Persons) Approach—This uses the thoughts of industry giants as the organizing structure. You might take, for instance, Dr. Deming's Seven Deadly Sins and use them as the basis for your remarks.

The FLP (Famous Living Persons) Approach—This uses the philosophies of one or more figures known to the audience. The person(s) may be organization- or industry-specific, as opposed to international figures, but his or her influence would serve as the basis for organizing your information.

The Problem-Solution Approach—Divided into two components, this is the most popular approach used in the business world today. Basically, it begins by delineating the problem and the possible ramifications that would ensue if the problem were not solved. The briefing or report would then go on to suggest several possible solutions and would conclude with a recommendation for corrective action.

The Order-of-Importance Approach—This approach discusses several related ideas and presents them in the order the speaker or writer has deemed most important. To illustrate, if you were discussing the benefits of the "open-book-management" style, you would begin with the most salient points first. (Some people prefer to "build up" to an impressive conclusion and so they do the reverse: they begin with the least significant details.)

The Deductive Approach—This begins with the premise or viewpoint or theory the presenter-of-information would like to focus on. The presenter would then proceed, quite literally, to *lead* the audience *from* this viewpoint into an understanding of the elements that constitute it.

The Inductive Approach—This is the reverse of the Deductive Approach. When we induce our audience, we literally *lead* them *into* our way of thinking through a deliberate argument that, we hope, builds to a convincing crescendo. If you wanted to prove that the current management gurus were simply "witch doctors," you would point out fallacies or weaknesses in their advice and conclude by calling them imposters.

The Topical Approach—This approach divides the topic into several components, none of which is more important than any of the others. If your topic, for instance, were "management," you could break that broad topic down into a number of components: management styles or management gurus, or changes facing managers, and so on.

There are many other ways to organize information, but these make the most frequent appearance in the world of business.

Procedure:

1. Show Slide 7-1 and keep it visible as you discuss the examples and also while participants are working on the assignment.

2. Ask them to pair up and choose one pattern of organization around which they will organize their thoughts in response to this prompt: "Tell me about your company (or agency, installation, firm, government unit, or organization represented by attendees)."

3. Allow about five minutes for selection of a pattern and for brainstorming.

4. Then ask participants to write a one- or two-paragraph essay telling about their company from the perspective of the pattern they have chosen.

5. After 15 or 20 minutes, call on a few pairs at random to share their essays. They could either identify the pattern they have selected or they could read the essay and then ask the class to tell what the pattern was.

Extending the Activity:

1. Halfway through the course, ask the class to summarize what they have learned, using one of the patterns provided.

2. Obtain copies of actual workplace documents and have participants analyze them to determine which pattern was used.

Workplace Connections:

1. Advise participants, if they have not already done so, to learn what organizational pattern their supervisors prefer to see in the reports they prepare. While problem-solution is the most frequently used in the world of business, varying circumstances may lead to varying preferences on the part of their supervisors.

2. Encourage participants to write the name of the pattern they are using at the top of draft copies of reports. When they see the pattern, they will be reminded of the kind of information to include and what information will be superfluous. Identifying the pattern in advance means the job of analysis is cut in half, for the structure virtually dictates the inclusions.

3. Suggest that participants try to determine what pattern was used the next time they listen to a speech by someone inside or outside the organization. Have them critically assess the effectiveness of this particular pattern. If it failed somehow, encourage participants to think about the pattern they would have used instead.

4. Collect a file full of magazine articles related to the topic of the training session or to subjects that are important to participants. Distribute one article to each participant and ask them to ascertain the pattern used in the article.

Questions for Further Consideration:

1. Are you consciously aware of using patterns as you do your writing at work? Why or why not?

2. Do you spend much time revising the structure of your business documents or presentations you have to make? If so, how could the use of patterns help?

3. What additional patterns of organization are useful to business writers?

4. Think about the best speech you have ever heard. What pattern was used?

Approaches to Organizing Information

Chronological

FDP (Famous Dead Persons)

FLP (Famous Living Persons)

Problem-Solution

Order of Importance

Deductive

Inductive

Topical

7-1

Overview:	Participants will first learn how to use this simple analytical tool and then apply it to given issues that affect us as corporate and community citizens.
Objective:	To encourage careful and deliberate scrutiny of issues prior to making decisions regarding them.
Supplies:	• Slide 8-1 • Equipment for displaying PowerPoint slides
Time:	Approximately 15 minutes
Advance Preparation:	If the training room allows flexible seating, arrange for table groups of 7 or 8 participants.
Participants/ Application:	Any number of participants can use this technique, for any number of issues that arise—either during the course of the training or afterwards in team and staff meetings. If used as a session-opener, the exercise will stimulate lively discussion among participants and so will quickly break the ice that exists among strangers. If used as a concluding activity, the exercise can focus on burning issues that arose during the training program.

Introduction to Concept:

When we think in a productive fashion, we are able to generalize solutions employed in comparable situations. (Reproductive thinking, by contrast, is merely learning or memorizing correct responses without being able to extend them to similar problems.) Superficial decision-making falls more into the reproductive category than the productive, for it is almost a rote response as opposed to a carefully considered response. [Show Slide 8-1.] There are numerous techniques that encourage thinking that goes beneath the surface. One such as the Pro Con'D model, which asks the problem-solver to consider:

Pro	—	What are the advantages to this particular issue?
Con	—	What are the disadvantages associated with this issue?
'D	—	What needs to be discussed further?

For example, if I asked, "How many of you think the minimum wage should be raised?" most of you would assert that indeed it should be raised. You would probably be able to cite advantages quite readily. Now let me ask, "Would you still want to raise it if I told you that research shows the drop-out rate increases when the minimum wage is increased?

The Pro Con'D approach puts a halt on our typical and understandable rush to judgment It forces us to weigh the various consequences that might result from a decision that initially seems quite appealing.

Procedure:

1. Divide the class into teams of six or seven members. Appoint a team leader for each team, whose job will be to ensure that the question has been put to Pro Con'D scrutiny before the "majority-rules" answer ("yes" or "no") is given.

2. Assign each team one of the following questions (or comparable ones of your own):

   1) Should we increase the minimum wage by $2.00?

   2) Should we prevent prisoners from filing frivolous lawsuits?

   3) Should there be guarantees given when employees are hired? (If so, what should they be?)

   4) Should judges instead of juries decide the outcomes of lawsuits?

   5) Should organization heads spend more time "walking the talk?"

   6) Should the word "secretary" be replaced with something else?

   7) Should juveniles committing adult crimes be tried as adults?

   8) Should there be a cap on athletes' salaries?

   9) Should there be mandatory training for all supervisors? (If so, what should it consist of?)

   10) Should there be a cap on the salaries of CEOs?

   11) Should our organization institute a "pay-for-knowledge" system?

   12) Should team leaders receive monetary compensation?

3. Allow 10 to 15 minutes for the Pro Con'D assessment of the issue.

4. Call on each group to share the answers they arrived at after the Pro Con'D discussion.

Extending the Activity:

1. Record issues on a flipchart as they arise throughout the training program. Periodically, use the Pro Con'D tool as a format for discussion prior to deciding on a feasible course of action.

2. Scan the newspaper for several days prior to the training program. Write the issues being debated on 3" x 5" cards—enough issues so each participant can have one. Have participants select a card, subject the issue to the Pro Con'D technique, and then discuss the issue with a partner, who will then share his or her Pro Con'D views on a different issue with the first person.

Workplace Connections:

1. There are "hot" topics in every workplace. Before you conclude the session, ask participants to write down five issues currently being debated at work. Then ask that they apply the Pro Con'D approach to these issues when they have time for reflection. After culling their own ideas, they should then engage others in a consideration of the issues before decisions are made about them.

2. Suggest that participants contact an arbitrator to learn how he or she is able to bring balance and equanimity of thought to situations that parties feel very strongly about.

Questions for Further Consideration:

1. How can we separate emotions from facts?

2. What has caused some of the arguments that have erupted in your workplace during the last six months?

3. What is the worst decision you ever made?

4. What factors surrounded the making of it?

5. As you reflect upon organizational decisions to proceed in one way or another, do you feel the evidence was given sufficient weight? Explain.

PRO —— What are the advantages to this particular issue?

CON —— What disadvantages are associated with this issue?

'D —— What needs to be discussed further?

8-1

Overview: Separated physically as well as by task, participants will write directions for their partners to follow. The directions ask them to draw a geometric design.

Objective: To foster analysis of a task and to determine the best way of directing others to perform that task.

Supplies: Handout 9-1 "A" for half the participants and "B" for the remaining half

Time: 25 minutes

Advance Preparation: Make copies of Handout 9-1 (half the number as the number of participants) and cut in half. The two halves of the room will work on two separate assignments. Seating should be arranged for this division.

Participants/ Application: This exercise will work with any number of participants. It is an excellent warm-up activity, but is also helpful when there has been a miscommunication between or among participants or between participants and facilitator. As a session-stimulator, it could be presented via a compliment: "You have managed to follow all the instructions I've presented thus far. However, I have been presenting instructions for a number of years. Let's see how well you can present instructions to a partner."

Introduction to Concept:

Following directions is easy if the person giving the directions has engaged in task-analysis first. Far too often, however, those who give instructions have not given thought to the best way of sharing knowledge. They have not planned in advance the most logical way to present important information.

Part of the "logic" associated with giving directions is the realization that there are numerous kinds of intelligence and numerous ways of absorbing information. Howard Gardner lists eight kinds—linguistic, logical, musical, spatial, kinesthetic, intrapersonal, interpersonal, and natural. J. P. Guilford has actually identified 124 separate and distinct kinds of intelligence; he regards them as a divisible cube of intellect.

The most efficient directions-giver appeals to the appropriate intelligence. If the intelligence is not known or if the audience has a combination of intelligences, the direction-giver appeals to more than one kind.

Procedure:

1. Physically arrange the room so that participants are sitting in one half of the room or the other. (If you do not have an even number of participants, the one "odd person out" will serve as the observer and will "float" around the room to make note of how this organization exercise was executed. The observer will make a report after the partners have conferred.)

2. Emphasize again the need to appeal to various modalities. Stress the fact that our backgrounds and experiences are different and while one person may recall geometric terms, for example, another may be thinking in terms of pies and pound cakes. And so, as good communicators, we need to express a given concept in more than one way.

3. Explain the task in the following manner: "Soon, I am going to give each of you a diagram. It is important not to let someone on the other side of the room see what you have. You are going to follow the instruction on the diagram, which essentially asks you to describe it in writing. There are certain words you cannot use.

4. Distribute Handout 9-1A to the left-hand side of the room and Handout 9-1B to the right-hand side of the room and give participants about 20 minutes to complete their written directions. They will use another sheet of paper, at the top of which they will have written their names.

5. Once they are finished, collect all the handouts, keeping the two piles separate.

6. Every person on the left-hand side will give his or her paper to a partner seated on the right-hand side and will receive a paper in return.

7. Class members will now draw a diagram based on the written instructions they were given.

8. When they are ready, you will ask the partners to sit together and to show each other their diagrams. As they do this, you will quickly give both handouts to each set of partners.

9. Give them an opportunity to compare their products to the original diagrams, stressing that the drawings should match the original exactly, including the thickness of lines and the size of the objects. Then ask each pair to decide what one thing in the directions would have improved the quality of the final product.

10. Call on each pair to share their improvement ideas as you compile a master list on chart paper.

Extending the Activity:

1. Have participants identify the criteria that constitute excellence in the giving of directions.

2. Work with them to prepare an assessment form incorporating those criteria, to be used to critique those who give instructions inside and outside the classroom.

Workplace Connections:

1. Encourage participants to "check for understanding" whenever they are given directions for completing a task that is new, difficult, or unclear to them. One of the simplest techniques they can employ is simply to paraphrase to the direction-giver their understanding of what they are to do.

2. The steps involved in the most important workplace processes should be made uniform and put into a procedural manual so that new hires or temporary replacements can work with little variation in the established processes.

Questions for Further Consideration:

1. What are some of the barriers to the effective exchange of instructions?

2. What do you think General George S. Patton meant when he said leaders should "give direction, not directions?"

3. What is the worst mistake you ever made as a result of unclear directions?

4. What would have prevented the mistake from occurring at all?

5. From whom in your lifetime have you learned the most? What made that person such an extraordinary teacher?

A. Study the following diagram carefully, because your goal is to have another person repro-
    duce it exactly. You cannot show it to that person. Nor can you use your hands—use only
    your words to describe it. (You will describe it in writing and your paper will then be turned
    over to your partner, who will try to reproduce what you were looking at, using only the
    directions you gave on paper.) One more rule: As you tell your partner how to draw this
    illustration, you **CANNOT USE** the words "circle" or "round" or "triangle." Good luck!

B. Study the following diagram carefully, because your goal is to have another person repro-
    duce it exactly. You cannot show it to that person. Nor can you use your hands—use only
    your words to describe it. (You will describe it in writing and your paper will then be turned
    over to your partner, who will try to reproduce what you were looking at, using only the
    directions you gave on paper.) One more rule: As you tell your partner how to draw this
    illustration, you **CANNOT USE** the words "circle" or "round" or "triangle." Good luck!

Overview: To stimulate thinking about steps in a process, participants will first work on a short ordering exercise, followed by a flowcharting activity, based on input from a volunteer.

Objective: To heighten awareness about processes and the factors leading to their improvement.

Supplies:
- Copies of Handout 10-1
- Slide 10-1
- Equipment for displaying PowerPoint slides

Time: 20–25 minutes

Advance Preparation: Make copies of Handout 10-1 for one-half the number of participants in the session. Half of the class will have Part A of the handout and the other half will receive Part B.

Participants/ Application: While this exercise works with any size group, too large a group might prevent those in the back of the room from seeing the work being done on the flipchart. With a large number of participants, seats could be arranged closer to the front for the second half of the exercise. Because the exercise usually provokes laughter, it makes an ideal warm-up. It also works as a session stimulator whenever the discussion focuses on work processes.

Introduction to Concept:

Flowcharting is now so popular as an analytic tool that the process is being taught in high schools throughout the country. Essentially, flowcharting forces us to analyze how work is done, step by step. Is it possible that two different people, performing the same process, might not be following the same steps? Could they follow the same steps, but not in the same order? [Pause. Elicit input.]

When we create a flowchart, we call upon our analytical skills to find the best sequence of order-steps, having first determined which steps add the most value.

Procedure:

1. Distribute Handout 10-1A to one-half of the class and 10-1B to the other. After a few moments, have them compare their results. Because A contains steps to be shared with experienced employees and B is written for newly hired employees, the steps—while the same for both groups—will probably be ordered differently.

2. Explain that many things must be considered before one decides how to sequence the steps in a process, including the nature of the audience receiving the information.

3. Next display Slide 10-1 showing the symbols used for flowcharting. While the slide is still being viewed, draw a simplified flow diagram on the flipchart:

Supervisor requests report for CEO

Gather data

Prepare report

Edit report

Submit to supervisor

Revision needed?...

... Revise

no/yes

... Send to CEO

4. Now ask a volunteer to come forward. Ask him or her to describe the steps involved in getting ready for work in the morning. Begin with the oval to show being awakened. (After the volunteer has mentioned what the specific input is—an alarm clock, for example—stop the exchange and address the group at large. Ask if everyone uses an alarm. The inputs will no doubt vary. Point out then that while the process of getting dressed in the morning has the same general steps for all of us, there is some variation. Next, make parallels with work processes. Discuss the fact that some people have found shortcuts, while others may be doing the work as they've been told to do it. Others may be doing it the way they think the supervisor wants it done. Help the group consider the benefit of comparing processes and of having some uniformity.

5. Then go directly to the output—the fully dressed person leaving the house on his or her way to work. Draw the symbol representing this on the bottom of the flipchart page.

6. Work with the volunteer now to determine the steps he or she takes to complete this process. As he or she supplies information, you will draw the flowchart, stopping periodically to ask questions. For example, "What do you do after you've done all the bathroom stuff?" If the volunteer says, "Then I jump into the shower," you will ask, "Should I put a box here to show 'Take off pajamas'?"

7. Conclude the activity by making further parallels to the workplace—we need to analyze the processes involved in our work tasks in order to determine where the greatest efficiency lies.

Extending the Activity:

1. Have participants work in pairs to explain to one another a process in which they engage at work. Once they have explained it verbally, they will explain it visually—drawing a flow diagram and then showing it to their partner. The partner will do the same with and for the first person.

2. A discussion of the real (as diagrammed in the preceding activity) compared to the ideal invariably yields important starting points in any quest for improvement. To draw the ideal flowchart, the partners ask each other, "What would this process look like if you could start from scratch, if you were given complete authority to design the process to be the most efficient sequence of steps?"

Workplace Connections:

1. Suggest that participants find someone within the workplace who is a "flowchart master." Have them learn as much as they can from that person or—better yet—have them ask that person to serve as an SME (subject matter expert), offering informal training for employees in flowcharting.

2. At staff meetings, employees could present flow diagrams of their most important processes and ask for ideas for streamlining the processes—perhaps once a week.

Questions for Further Consideration:

1. To what extent have the work processes in your workplace been standardized?

2. What causes us to be stuck in our ways and stuck in the ways we work?

3. If you wished to encourage your co-workers to improve the way work is done, what would you do first?

4. How would an understanding of the different ways different employees do the same work benefit the work unit?

5. What could you learn by flowcharting the most critical of your work processes?

A. You have been asked to lead a group, composed of experienced employees, in a discussion of ways to make their daily work processes more efficient. How would you organize the following points? In what order would you recommend they be done on a daily basis? Write the number "1" beside the item you would stress first, "2" beside the item you consider second-most important as they organize their day, and so on.

    a. _____ Check your to-do list from the preceding day.

    b. _____ Check with your manager to learn if he or she has priorities you must attend to.

    c. _____ Check your e-mail.

    d. _____ Tackle your top priority and get it done before doing anything else.

    e. _____ Remember that internal and external customers are the reason we work.

    f. _____ Make important phone calls and get them out of the way.

    g. _____ Check with co-workers to see if there are any meetings scheduled or other important group/team assignments that you should be working on.

B. You have been asked to lead a group, composed of newly-hired employees, in a discussion of ways to make their daily work processes more efficient. How would you organize the following points? In what order would you recommend they be done on a daily basis? Write the number "1" beside the item you would stress first, "2" beside the item you consider second-most important as they organize their day, and so on.

    a. _____ Check your to-do list from the preceding day.

    b. _____ Check with your manager to learn if he or she has priorities you must attend to.

    c. _____ Check your e-mail.

    d. _____ Tackle your top priority and get it done before doing anything else.

    e. _____ Remember that internal and external customers are the reason we work.

    f. _____ Make important phone calls and get them out of the way.

    g. _____ Check with co-workers to see if there are any meetings scheduled or other important group/team assignments that you should be working on.

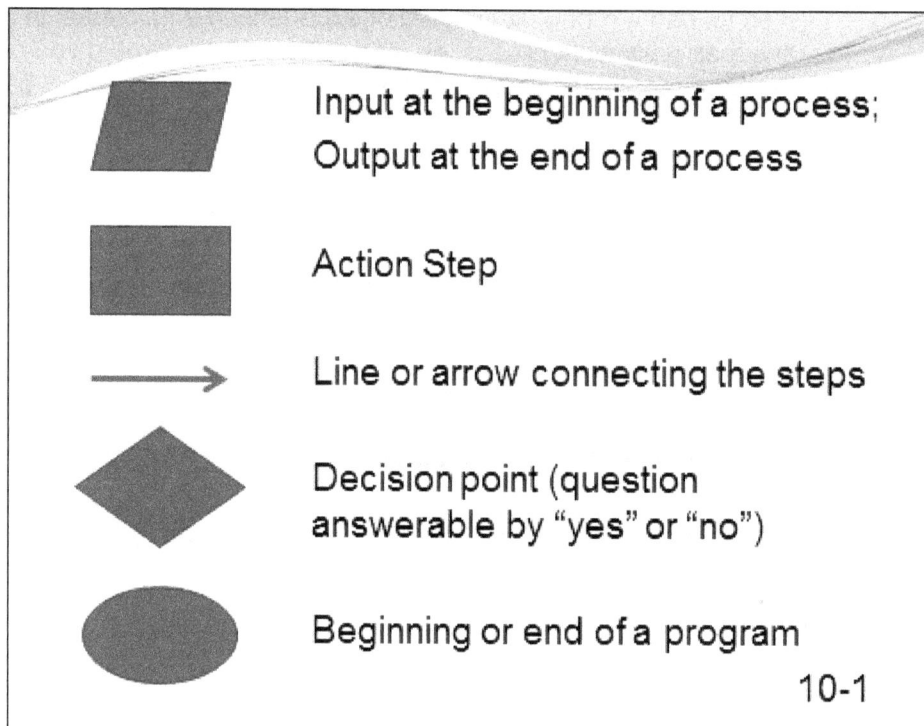

Input at the beginning of a process; Output at the end of a process

Action Step

Line or arrow connecting the steps

Decision point (question answerable by "yes" or "no")

Beginning or end of a program

10-1

Overview: Starting with a problem best solved by actually envisioning the situations, participants will proceed to contemplate a work-related problem in the same fashion.

Objective: To foster imaginative reasoning.

Supplies: A "back-up" problem—in case some class members have seen the original sock problem before. This will suffice:

> *You have six matches and must form four equal-sided triangles from them.*

When you are tutoring the "imagine" group, encourage them to think in three dimensions, not two. If they can, they will have a flat triangle and in the space above it, three intersecting matches meeting to make three additional triangles.

Time: Approximately 20 minutes

Advance Preparation: If possible, arrange for a breakout room so that half the class can work with you in solving a problem and the other half can leave the room to work on the same problem collectively or individually.

Participants/ Application: This exercise, suitable for any number of participants, works especially well as an ice-breaker, forcing communal effort and collegiality. It can also serve as a preview to the many times during the training to follow that participants will need to engage in this sort of reasoning as various issues are addressed.

The exercise can also be used as a summarizing activity: have pairs imagine what it will be like when they return to their work sites. They can then formulate an action plan that will enable them to apply the learning they have acquired to the all-too-real circumstances awaiting them.

Introduction to Concept:

Einstein as a child used to imagine himself chasing sunbeams through space. He often spoke of the importance of fantasizing. He regarded imagination, in fact, as being "more important than knowledge." In more contemporary terms, management expert Tom Peters refers to imagination as "the only source of real value in the new economy." In the following example, the answer will come more easily if you can actually imagine yourself performing the action.

> *You have just put a load of socks into the clothes dryer. There are 10 black socks and 10 brown socks inside the dryer. Without actually looking at what you are pulling out, how many socks will you have to take out of the dryer before you have a pair that matches?*

Procedure:

1. Divide the class in half but assure participants that both teams are working on the same problem.

2. Gather one group around you and explain that you are not going to tell them the answer, but you are going to suggest that they try to find that answer by imaging themselves actually pulling socks out of the dryer, one at a time. How many socks would they need before finding a matched pair?

3. Review the answers with participants and encourage them to describe the process (if any) they used to solve the problem. Discuss how visualization could have helped (for example: You've bent over and pulled out a sock, but you cannot look at it. What color could it be? (Brown or Black.) Now you bend down and pull out another. What color is this one? (Brown or Black.) Pull out one more sock. What color is this? (Brown or Black.) What possibilities now exist with the three socks you have before you? (All three brown or all three black or two black and one brown or two brown and one black.) No matter the scenario, if you have three, you will have a matching pair.

4. Now divide the class into teams of four or five. Ask each team to select some change they are currently facing or would like to introduce (preferably work-related). Another option is for them to consider some danger or crisis situation in the workplace. Have them visualize, step-by-step, the events that could lead to various possible outcomes. Then have them retrace those steps, specifying how they would prepare for such crisis-possibilities.

5. Call on one person from each team to share the group's imaginative reasoning.

Extending the Activity:

1. To develop spatial reasoning via visualization, prepare a number of exercises like this one:

    What will this figure look like if it is rotated or turned over? Encourage visualization to find the answer.

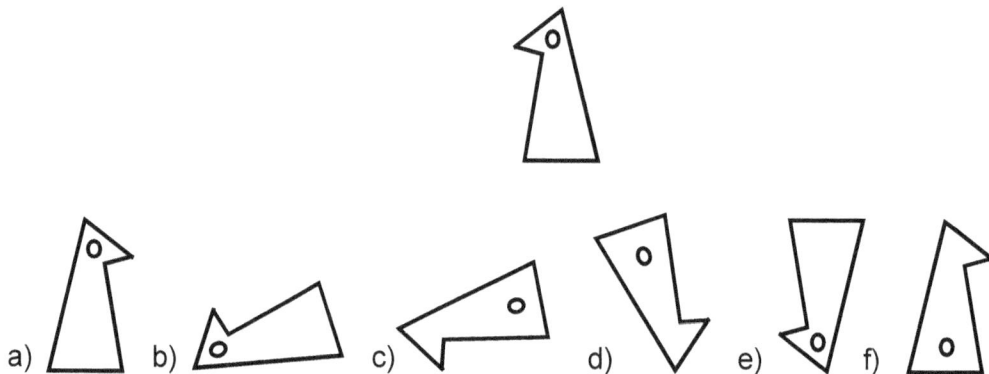

The answer is b) (rotated) and if you wish to make it really difficult, the answer for turned over and upside-down is e).

2. The gift of fantasy, which Einstein also valued, can work for any of us. The fantasizing process would be as simple as imagining the perfect workplace, the perfect job, the perfect friendship, etc., specifying the elements that create the perfection, and then working to achieve some or all of them. Lead participants through such a process in relation to a situation that parallels one of the most serious discussions that arose during the training day.

Workplace Connections:

1. Encourage employees to continue their imaginative reasoning after the training is over. Using the buddy system, they can each prepare visual challenges like the first one in the extended activity. Then, on a daily basis, they can exchange their ten with those prepared by another employee. Depending on how many employees are involved, participants could have a whole month's worth of challenges. Once all have been given and received, participants could prepare another ten and continue in the same way.

2. Recommend that participants read biographies of those they consider outstanding leaders and/or visionaries. Once a month, members of the informal group could have lunch together and discuss what they heave learned about calculation-via-conjecture.

Questions for Further Consideration:

1. What value can individuals derive from sharpening their imaginative reasoning abilities?

2. What major changes do you see in your future? What preparations are you making so the transitions between current and future states will be facilitated?

3. How much daydreaming do you do? Has it ever led to an improved state of affairs?

4. What can you do to improve your imaginative-reasoning abilities?

Overview: After being presented with an example, participants will apply the Five-Why technique to a current workplace problem and then to a situation involving recent news events.

Objective: To allow participants to practice the Five-Why technique.

Supplies: Copies of a recent news article, one per participant

Time: About 20 minutes

Advance Preparation: Make copies of a recent news report that invites in-depth analysis. If you can, arrange seating so table groups of five or six can work together.

Participants/ Application: Any number of participants can work on this exercise, which works best as a mid-session or end-of-session skill-builder. By the halfway point in the course (or by the end), enough provocative questions or issues will have arisen to warrant the Five-Why application.

Introduction to Concept:

A popular problem-solving tool from the world of Total Quality Management (TQM) is the Five-Why technique. It has one person continuing to ask "Why?" until the root cause of a problem has been uncovered. This example shows how continued questioning helps us to analyze the multiple factors involved in problems, and not just the most obvious, most superficial ones.

William's variance report is late.

Why?

He's always playing catch up.

Why?

He's been assigned to a two-week training program during the middle of budgets.

Why?

He really needs the training.

Why?

He was never given an orientation program when he was first hired.

Why?

I guess he just slipped through the cracks.

With this kind of probing, it is much easier to uncover the root cause of the problem. And that root cause, as we saw in William's case, may well go beyond the circumstances of the particular problem being investigated. While the lateness of a given report may be serious, more serious is the problem of employees not having the training they need to do the job *before* they start to do that job. The slipping-through-the-cracks problem is the long-term one that needs immediate attention.

Procedure:

1. Working in teams of five or six, participants will record problems that occur/exist in the workplace or in any other context they wish to address.

2. They will probe beneath the surface of the problem (as originally stated) to attempt to learn the real cause and, thus, what might be the real solution.

3. A representative (or two representatives, if there are only a few teams) from each team will meet with other representatives to prepare a report on what the various teams learned. As this special team is working, the remaining participants will work on a second exercise—applying the Five-Why technique to a recent news story in an effort to uncover beneath-the-surface causes for a given effect. Distribute the news story.

4. After 10 or 15 minutes, ask for the two reports: the first by a spokesperson for the special team and the second by a spokesperson from the team that discussed the recent news story.

Extending the Activity:

1. Invite a guest speaker (a senior manager, a community leader, a police officer) to address the class about a common problem. An appointed spokesperson from the class will ask (as professionally and diplomatically as possible) five "Why?" questions to get beneath surface discussions.

2. Ask participants to think about the last five major problems they solved or decisions they made. Have them discuss with one or two others the depth to which they probed beneath the surface to find root causes of the problems.

Workplace Connections:

1. Recommend that employees use the Five Why technique the next time they are tempted to hurl an accusation at a co-worker. Instead of jumping to conclusions and saying things they might later regret, participants can use the five "Why" questions as a means of exploring the problem instead of attacking the person with the problem.

2. Suggest that participants share this technique with their supervisors for future use.

Questions for Further Consideration:

1. What is causing some of the communication problems in your workplace?

2. Specifically, how should managers deal with employees who have problems?

3. What might be a negative result of such probing?

Overview: First, participants will generate a list of workplace problems. Then, they will examine possible solutions by viewing the problems from a perspective that is at odds with the typical response.

Objective: To develop analytic thought by examining opposites.

Supplies:
- Slide 13-1
- Equipment for displaying PowerPoint slides
- Flipchart—ideally one for each team of four or five participants

Time: 15–20 minutes

Advance Preparation: If the seating is flexible enough, arrange it to accommodate groups of 4 or 5 participants.

Participants/ Application: Any number of participants can work on this exercise, which can be used as a session opener (to preview the issues that will likely arise during the training). It can also be used as either a session-stimulator or summary exercise to stimulate discussion around problems that have been cited or concerns that have been expressed in relation to the topic of the training session.

Introduction to Concept:

The Chinese philosopher Lao-Tzu, born 600 B.C., advised his followers to "learn to see things backward, inside out, and upside down." When we follow this advice, we can embrace opposing or conflicting views and find within them a sensible path to pursue. We can free ourselves from traditional thought patterns by welcoming new and unexplored possibilities.

For example, ever since murder mysteries have been written, authors have waited until the very last chapter to solve the mystery, keeping the reader or viewer wondering about the murderer's identity. In the early eighties, however, two writers decided to "see things backwards." Levinson and Link revealed the murderer's identity in the first few moments of the story and lo and behold, Detective Columbo was born.

Other examples reflective of Lao-Tzu's long-ago recommendation include:

- The current corporate trend of having employees evaluate their managers instead of having the managers alone do the evaluating.

- The successful software company that decided to increase its profits by actually giving its software away.

- The development of the electric car as a solution to the problem of rising oil prices.

Procedure:

1. Have participants work in teams of four or five to list 20 to 30 problems that face us as members of a business community (or even as adults, as parents, as neighbors, as Americans, as parishioners, as citizens of the global village, etc.).

2. Next, they will generate several atypical perspectives for each of the problems—the approach is "upside-down" compared to the one usually used; the problem is tackled "backward;" and the problem-solvers are "inside out" the circle ordinarily chosen to confront the problem.

3. Then, they will work with their Lao-Tzu-type ideas to see how many of them can be fashioned into possible solutions for the problems identified.

4. Spokespersons from each team will report on their work.

Extending the Activity:

1. Creativity guru Edward DeBono declares, "Of one thing we can be sure: the quality of our life in the future will be determined by the quality of our thinking in the present." His words echo those of Albert Einstein, who wryly noted, "We live in a world of problems which can no longer be solved by the level of thinking which created them." Show Slide 13-1 and lead a discussion based on these quotations shown on the slide. Elicit examples from current events to illustrate their basic thrust.

2. Ask small groups of participants to outline a commencement address they would make on the topic of problems the graduates will face and the level of thinking needed to solve them.

Workplace Connections:

1. Suggest that participants in their next staff or team meeting first appoint an observer and then lead the discussion of an issue by having co-workers examine the situation backwards, inside out, and upside down. Following the discussion, have the observer compare the results of this opposite-exploration to the results achieved in the usual way.

2. A study of 2,000 computer programmers found that those whose hobbies included working puzzles and playing logic games performed best on the job. No matter what position we hold within our organizations, we can all benefit from having our analytical skills honed. Ask for a volunteer to form a Puzzle-Solvers Club at work.

Questions for Further Consideration:

1. What artists do you know who have looked at things backwards, inside out, and upside down?

2. How can this kind of thinking be extended to the workplace?

3. Who is the best problem-solver in your workplace? What is his or her style?

4. What kinds of problems are best solved using this kind of analysis?

Edward DeBono:

"Of one thing we can be sure: the quality of our life in the future will be determined by the quality of our thinking in the present."

Albert Einstein:

"We live in a world of problems which can no longer be solved by the level of thinking which created them."

13-1

Overview: After exposure to two interesting problems, participants will employ the Force-Field Analysis to focus their thinking on resources that could be tapped in the process of solving a given problem.

Objective: To develop the use of analytical thinking via a structured format.

Supplies:
- Flipchart
- Marking pens

Time: Approximately 25 minutes

Advance Preparation: Draw the Force Field Analysis (as shown in step 4 of the procedure) on the flipchart but keep it covered until the appropriate time.

Participants/ Application: This exercise works with any size group at any point when a cerebral energizer is needed. The exercise can be used to begin a session if a question like this is posed to the group: "What do you envision as the ideal state of affairs as far as [name topic of course you are facilitating] is concerned?" The analysis required by the Force Field Tool can also be related to various discussions that arise during the course of the day. If used as an end-of-session exercise, the question for the group would be, "Where do we go from here?" This question will lead to the broad division of forces (both restraining and driving) that will help participants achieve an ideal state.

Introduction to Concept:

Often, we fail to find the solutions we need because we fail to use the resources we have. We wear blinders, it seems, that prevent us from using what is right in front of us or right inside of us. Or we impose imaginary limits upon ourselves and assume that we are not allowed to proceed in a particular fashion. In truth, though, there are fewer rules or impediments than we think there are.

A good example of how available resources aren't always used to solve an important problem is this one involving a creative engineering class at M.I.T. The instructor had placed two ping-pong balls at the bottom of a metal cylinder, which was bolted to the floor of the science lab. The cylinder was about seven inches wide and about five feet high. The students had one full hour to remove the ping-pong balls from the cylinder. They could not leave the room but were free to use anything in the room. The professor encouraged them to work together, reminding them that if they found a solution, they would all pass the final exam and if they did not, they would all fail. They all failed. Had you been in that room, how would you have solved the problem? [Pause. Elicit solutions.]

Procedure:

1. The answer to the M.I.T. problem is "water," which students could have taken from the faucets in order to float the balls to the top. After challenging the class with the M.I.T. problem, ask participants to solve this next problem. [**Note:** It is important to set up this problem by using a colored magic marker to draw the lines and a different color to draw the letters.

    In the following diagram, which letter does not belong?

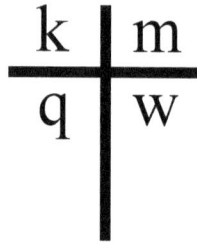

$$\begin{array}{c|c} k & m \\ \hline q & w \end{array}$$

2. Call on various participants to explain their answers and then give the correct one: The letter "t," which most people don't even "see," is out of place because it is bigger, thicker, and of a different color than the other letters.

3. Psychologist Kurt Lewin devised a problem-solving tool that asks us to consider the current state of affairs and to juxtapose it with an ideal state of affairs. Having done that, we now consider what driving forces (indicated by a plus sign) will help us achieve the idealized state by using existing resources. Next, we think about the restraining forces (depicted by a minus sign) that may be preventing us from achieving the desired conditions.

4. Continue with this mini-lecture:

    The Force Field Analysis is depicted as a large "T," as you can see here. [Show diagram on flipchart.] It's a valuable tool for analyzing a problem, ascertaining its causes, and evaluating the resources available for achieving the desired effect. An example of a problem that might be subject to such analysis is the illiteracy rate in America—1 out of 5 adults is functionally illiterate. That is the current status; ideally, there would be no such thing as illiteracy. The next step involves asking what forces could be used to bring us to the ideal state. Finally, we would consider what forces are causing the rate to be so high or keeping us from reaching the idea. By reviewing the two columns, we can next decide the course of action that should be pursued.

Current state:	*20% illiteracy*	
Ideal state:	*100% literacy*	

Driving Forces (+)	Restraining Forces (-)
government intervention *volunteer program* *public service ads* *athletes as mentors* *involvement of business* *community*	*busy lives* *too much television* *high dropout rates* *single parent homes* *immigration*

5. Divide the class into small groups of four or five and give each team a sheet of chart paper. Have each group identify a problem at the top of the chart paper and report its current and ideal states. The problem could be one currently facing them as businesspeople or us all as a society.

6. Give each group another group's chart paper and ask members to list both the Driving and the Restraining forces for the problem listed.

7. After about 15 minutes, return the papers to the original groups and ask them to add further Driving and Restraining forces and then to select the one force (in either column) that—if they could direct their energies to it—they think could most effect the ideal solution.

8. Call on a spokesperson from each team to report on their selection.

Extending the Activity:

1. Have participants interview one another to learn what special talents/knowledge/abilities they have. Keep a classroom or corporate list of these resources and draw upon various individuals at various times for various projects.

2. Periodically do a brief force field analysis of issues raised by participants that relate to the subject matter of the course.

3. Begin the class with a large force field analysis addressing this issue: *"How can we maximize the investment in training, after the training?"* The current research is discouraging: Less than half of participants in training programs return to work and effect changes based on the new learning they have acquired. The ideal, of course, would be to have every participant put to use the new skills/concepts they acquired immediately after their return to the workplace.

4. Begin a collection of instances when slavish adherence to rules results in loss to an individual or organization. For example, after transferring to a new school in Seattle, a youngster asked his parents if he could go back to his old school. The reason for his request: The new school did not permit boys to work in the library. The no-boys rule meant considerable intellectual loss for the new school because... the fourth-grader who returned to View Ridge was none other than Bill Gates!

Workplace Connections:

1. If participants have not been asked by their supervisors, "What is the greatest contribution you can make to this organization?" encourage them to at least ask the question of co-workers or team members with whom they work.

2. We sometimes overlook available resources because we have not tapped the wealth of historical precedents. Suggest that participants study what has gone before in order to accomplish what is yet to be. In other words, what has been done in the past that might facilitate the solutions currently being sought or implemented?

Questions for Further Consideration:

1. What rules do you feel should be changed?

2. What do you think Tom Peters means when he says, "If you have gone a whole week without being disobedient, you are doing yourself and your organization a disservice?"

3. What resources—human and other—remain untapped in your organization?

4. Do you agree with author James Fixx, who asserts, "In solving puzzles, a self-assured attitude is half the battle?"

5. Kurt Lewin, originator of the Force Field Analysis method, has a model of change that calls for "Thawing," "Changing," and "Refreezing." Assume you wanted to make some positive change in the workplace. How, what, where, when, and possibly who would you thaw, change, and refreeze?

Overview:	"Autonomy of object" refers to the problem-solving process of making a problem come alive in order to find a possible solution. Participants will work in small groups to solve a problem of their own choosing in this manner.
Objective:	To provide participants with a problem-solving tool.
Supplies:	None required
Time:	Approximately 15 minutes
Advance Preparation:	Arrange the group, if logistics permit, into subgroups of five members.
Participants/ Application:	Because this exercise generates lively discussion, it works well as an ice-breaking activity. Applicable to any size group, it can also be used during the training session or at its conclusion. All that is needed for these last two applications would be a problem that arose naturally during the preceding training.

Introduction to Concept:

"Autonomy of object" is a technique requiring the problem-solver to actually personify the problem by placing it in the context of a different time or a different place. Interesting and novel solutions to the problem are frequently embedded within the mental associations we normally make with a particular era.

Let us say that graffiti is a problem in a given neighborhood. If the problem were personified, the graffiti might be seen as a bandit in the Wild West era. The Wild West might make you think of a "posse," and conceivably a posse would be formed to patrol the neighborhood looking for the offenders. This scenario might also make you think of sheriffs. By extension, then, perhaps the police could be asked to patrol more often than they currently do, or could be turned to for advice. Wild west-thinking might also lead you to badges, with their shiny, reflective surfaces. These thoughts could result in an invitation to a chemist to discuss chemicals that might be sprayed on select surfaces to deflect the paint.

Procedure:

1. Begin by listing numerous problems on the board or flipchart. Use problems related to workplace issues, if possible.

2. Prepare a second list, with input from participants, of various eras/locations different from the present. For each era and location, free-associate words related to those times and places.

3. Divide the class into small groups next and ask participants to select a problem and an era or location. They will then devise a possible solution by making the problem come alive (as was done with the graffiti-as-bandit situation).

4. Have the groups share their solutions.

Extending the Activity:

1. Have a current copy of the local newspaper available. Distribute a section or several pages to each group. Ask them to use the autonomy-of-object procedure to make the problem come alive and then to identify a lively solution for the problem.

2. Discuss the simple technique of *personification,* which makes an inanimate object come alive. Extend the discussion to workplace situations by asking participants to first list issues that concern them, and then to regard those issues from a new perspective by completing one or more of the following prompts:

   "If this problem could talk, it would say…"
   "If this problem could think, it would realize…"
   "If this problem could hear, it would have known…"
   "If this problem could create, it would have made…"
   "If this problem could be dressed, it would look like…"

Workplace Connections:

1. Ask a group of five supervisors/managers to volunteer to do the following: They will use the autonomy-of-object technique to ameliorate a workplace situation. Then, they will report back to their respective subordinates the success they had with the technique. If it worked well for them, encourage the supervisors to occasionally solve problems this way with their subordinates.

2. A genius has been defined as someone who shoots at something nobody else can see—and hits it. To generate this kind of visionary thinking, ask for a volunteer to call participants at least once during the next six months with this question, *"What are you looking at that no one else can see?"* To be sure, there are no guarantees that such prodding will result in lively solutions. But it may very well increase the number of invisible targets being hit.

Questions for Further Consideration:

1. The autonomy-of-object technique works because it stimulates thoughts we would not have had without the special context in which we place the problem. What other techniques do you know of to stimulate free association or brainstorming?

Overview: After studying several examples of innovation spurred by a pet peeve, participants will list things that bother them. Then, in pairs, they will seek solutions to the items listed by others.

Objective: To encourage "paradigm-shifts" so that problems can be viewed as sources of invention, instead of obstacles.

Supplies: 3" x 5" cards

Time: About 25 minutes

Advance Preparation: If possible, arrange seating so pairs can work together.

Participants/ Application: This exercise is flexible enough for use at various points during the training day. Because it encourages the sharing of personal annoyances, it makes a good ice-breaker. If the annoyances are related to the topic of the training or to industry trends, the exercise can then be used as an energizer or as a means of bringing closure to the class.

Introduction to Concept:

"Necessity," it has been repeatedly said, "is the mother of invention." Need *is* a necessary condition, but it is not enough innovation. From time to time, we have all been troubled by a particular event or personal encounter or circumstance. Consciously or subconsciously, we recognize the need for something to be different in order for the event, encounter, or circumstance to be improved. But until we spend the necessary time remedying the situations, the inventiveness will not be born.

History is filled with inventors and innovators who took a need and gave it the time and energy required for breakthroughs to occur. Here are but a few examples:

- Edwin Land, while vacationing in Santa Fe, New Mexico, took a photograph of his five-year-old daughter, Jennifer, who promptly asked, "Can I see the picture, Daddy?" When he answered "No," she demanded to know why not. Her question intrigued him. Why *not* invent a camera that could develop film within its own mechanism, he thought, and produce the finished photo in a matter of minutes? In time, this family need became the Polaroid Land Camera.

- George De Mestral was a Swiss mechanical engineer who loved to go hunting in the mountains of his homeland. After returning home one day, he began to remove the burrs that had stuck to his wool pants. He was surprised at the difficulty he had knocking them loose. Under a microscope, he saw the burrs were composed of hundreds of tiny hooks. Within ten years, he had patented Velcro, now used to keep the feet of astronauts stuck to the floor in zero-gravity conditions and in hundreds of other situations.

- While skating outdoors near his home in Farmington, Maine, a teenager named Chester Greenwood discovered that his ears were literally turning blue. The need to protect himself from the cold resulted in the invention of ear muffs, a patent for which he obtained at age 18.

- Brian Margolis was always annoyed by the difficulty he had maneuvering an empty plate through a buffet line, while he had a drink in one hand and the plate in the other. Margolis subsequently invented Plate-Mate, a plastic device that can be attached to the dinner plate, allowing you one free hand for filling your plate.

- Dr. Kelly Tucker, a cardiologist at the University of California at San Francisco, has filed a patent application for a suction cup invention to assist in the administration of CPR. Tucker's invention was inspired by a toilet plunger, which a young man used in an emergency to compress and decompress his father's chest during a heart attack.

- Art Fry, a scientist for 3M, was troubled by the bits of paper he stuck in his hymnal while singing in the church choir. The little scraps, intended to keep his place, would fall out and cause him to constantly *lose* his place. Fry experimented with putting adhesive on the little scraps of paper and Post-it Notes were born.

Procedure:

1. Distribute a 3" x 5" card to each participant and ask for 5–10 examples of things that annoy, bother, or bug them. Ask them to recall times when they said, "Somebody really ought to..." or "Someone should come up with a way..." or "There must be a better way to..." (Ideally, their complaints will be work-related, but that's not necessary.) Then allow 5 to 10 minutes of quiet time for participants to recall their personal peeves or bugaboos. [Fill out a card yourself.]

2. Collect the cards. As you do so, have participants select a partner with whom to work.

3. Distribute two cards to each pair and ask them to find a solution to one of the problems presented.

4. After 10 to 15 minutes, call on each pair to share their innovative thinking.

Extending the Activity:

1. Form a focus group of customers (internal or external) and have them report to the class about a company product or service they use—one provided by an internal "supplier." Their comments should address the "What-bugs-you" question as well as these four:

   1) What are we doing that you like?

   2) What are we doing that you don't like?

   3) What are we not doing that you wish we were doing?

   4) What are we doing that you wish we weren't?

2. Invite the organization's CEO to address the need for innovative thinking that will keep the organization competitive in the years ahead.

Workplace Connections:

1. Suggest that participants interview old-timers, those revered individuals with 30+ years of service in the same organization. They should ask the long-term employees about the origin of the work processes in which employees now engage. They should also ask how things have changed, what caused the changes, and how difficult it has been to adapt to change.

2. Encourage employees to speak with those in charge of the organization's suggestion program (and to institute such a program if none exists). They should try to determine which ideas proved to be most profitable for the organization and what the genesis for those ideas was.

Questions for Further Consideration:

1. What improvements have you made at work or at home because of a situation that caused you to say, "There must be a better way?"

2. What is the best invention that you know of that was born of necessity?

3. What "idea-toxins" exist in most environments?

4. What "self-talk" is needed to prevent us from being our own worst critics?

5. For how long have you been doing your most important work in exactly the same way? Explain why it is too long or when you think it will be necessary to change the way that work is now done.

Bibliography

Adams, James. *Conceptual Blockbusting.* New York: Addison-Wesley, 1986.

Albrecht, Karl. *Brain Power.* New York: Prentice-Hall, Inc., 1980.

Armstrong, David. *Managing by Storying Around.* New York: Doubleday, 1992.

Bennis, Warren and Burt Nanus. *Leaders: The Strategies for Taking Charge.* New York: Harper & Row, 1985.

Bridge, William. *Job Shift.* New York: Addison-Wesley, 1995.

Campbell, David. *Take the Road to Creativity and Get Off Your Dead End.* Greensboro: Center for Creative Leadership, 1977.

Drucker, Peter. *The Effective Executive.* New York: Harper & Row, 1985.

Foster, Richard. *Innovation.* New York: Simon & Schuster, 1986.

Hammer, Michael and James Champy. *Reengineering the Corporation.* New York: HarperCollins, 1993.

Imai, Masaaki. *Kaizen.* New York: Random House, 1986.

Kriegel, Robert. *If It Ain't Broke, Break It!* New York: Time Warner, 1991.

McClelland, David. *Some Social Consequences of Achievement Motivation.* New York: Irvington Publishers, Inc., 1993.

Munk, Nina and Suzanne Oliver. "Think Fast." *Forbes* magazine, Volume 160, Number 3, March 24, 1997, pages 146–151.

Naisbitt, John and Patricia Aburdene. *Megatrends 2000.* New York: William Morrow & Company, 1990.

Nelson, Robert. *1001 Ways to Reward Employees.* New York: Workman Publishers, 1994.

Norins, Hanley. *Traveling Creative Workshop.* New York: Prentice Hall, 1990.

Quinlivan-Hall, David and Peter Renner. *In Search of Solutions.* Vancouver: PFR Training Associates Limited, 1990.

Ruggiero, Vincent. *The Art of Thinking.* New York: Harper & Row, 1988.

Stack, Jack. *The Great Game of Business.* New York: Doubleday, 1992.

Thompson, Charles. *What a Great Idea.* New York: HarperCollins, 1992.

Wallenchinsky, David and Amy Wallace. *The Book of Lists.* New York: Little, Brown and Company, 1993.